Chapter 1.

Tips for Seniors and Anyone Cooking for One:

1.1. The Joy of Cooking for Yourself

1.2. The Importance of a Nutritious Breakfast

1.3. Maintaining a Healthy Breakfast Routine

1.4. Encouragement for Trying New Recipes

1.5. Cooking Tips and Kitchen Safety for Seniors

1.1. "The Joy of Cooking for Yourself"

is all about creating delicious and satisfying meals for one. Cooking for yourself can be a joyful and rewarding experience, allowing you to experiment with flavours, ingredients, and techniques at your own pace.

Here's a step-by-step guide to help you get started:

1. Plan Your Meals:

Take some time to plan your meals for the week. Consider your dietary preferences, nutritional needs, and any special occasions.

2. Stock Your Kitchen:

Make sure your kitchen is well-stocked with essential ingredients such as grains, pasta, canned goods, spices, oils, and fresh produce.

Invest in quality cookware and utensils that make cooking easier and more enjoyable.

3. Portion Control:

When cooking for yourself, it's essential to portion your ingredients correctly to avoid food waste. Use measuring cups and a kitchen scale if needed.

4. Batch Cooking:

Cook larger batches of your favourite dishes and freeze individual portions for later use. This can save you time on busy days.

5. Plan Balanced Meals:

Aim for balanced meals that include a protein source, vegetables, and carbohydrates. This ensures you get a variety of nutrients in your diet.

6. Embrace Leftovers:

Don't be afraid to enjoy leftovers. They can make quick and easy meals on days when you don't feel like cooking from scratch.

7. Try New Recipes:

Experiment with new recipes and cuisines to keep your meals exciting. There are plenty of cookbooks, websites, and cooking apps with single-serving recipes.

8. Cooking Techniques:

Learn different cooking techniques like sautéing, roasting, grilling, and steaming to add variety to your meals.

9. Mindful Eating:

Practice mindful eating by savouring your meals and paying attention to flavours and textures. This can enhance your dining experience.

10. Grocery Shopping:

Plan your grocery shopping efficiently by making a list and sticking to it. This helps reduce food waste and saves money.

11. Prep Ahead:

On your free days, do some meal preparation. Chop vegetables, marinate proteins, or prepare sauces in advance to streamline cooking during the week.

12. Stock a Well-Planned Pantry:

Maintain a well-organised pantry with staples like rice, beans, canned tomatoes, and spices. This ensures you always have the basics on hand.

13. Food Storage:

Invest in good-quality food storage containers to store leftovers and ingredients. Label and date items to prevent waste.

14. Enjoy the Process:

Cooking for yourself can be a therapeutic and enjoyable experience. Put on your favourite music or podcast, and take your time in the kitchen.

15. Share with Others:

Invite friends or family over for a meal occasionally. It's an excellent way to socialize and share your culinary creations.

Remember that cooking for yourself is not only about nourishment but also about self-care and creativity. It's an opportunity to explore your tastes, improve your culinary skills, and enjoy the pleasure of a well-prepared meal. So, embrace "The Joy of Cooking for Yourself" and make it your own culinary adventure!

1.2. The importance of a Nutritious Breakfast for Seniors Living Alone.

A healthy breakfast is a fundamental aspect of senior nutrition, particularly for those living alone. It provides essential nutrients, sustains energy levels, maintains physical health, boosts the immune system supports cognitive function, promotes emotional well-being, encourages healthy eating habits, offers social and emotional benefits, and aids in weight management. Encouraging seniors to prioritise breakfast as a vital part of their daily routine, to enjoy a better quality of life and overall health, allows them to age gracefully and independently. Caregivers, family members, and communities can play a role in ensuring that seniors have access to nutritious breakfast options and the support they need to maintain a healthy lifestyle.

As individuals age, their nutritional needs change, and many of their habits too, particularly if they are living alone. One of the most crucial dietary habits for seniors, and indeed for people of all ages, is having healthy and nutritious breakfasts. Making it essential to emphasize the importance of nutritious breakfast. A well balanced breakfast is important for maintaining overall health and quality of life in the elderly population. The recipes and this book will explore and highlight the significance of a healthy and nutritious breakfast for seniors who are living independently.

Here are those fundamental nutrition benefits in greater detail:

1. Provides Essential Nutrients:

A nutritious breakfast is an excellent source of essential vitamins, health, muscle strength, and overall well-being. For seniors who may be at higher risk of nutrient deficiencies, a balanced breakfast is a valuable source of these nutrients.

2. Boosts Energy Levels:

Starting the day with a healthy breakfast helps seniors maintain steady energy levels, allowing them to stay active and engaged throughout the day. After a night's sleep , the body requires a source of fuel to kickstart metabolism and cognitive function; fuel to function optimally. Skipping breakfast can lead to fatigue and reduced productivity, which can be especially challenging for seniors living alone who may need to perform various daily tasks without assistance.

3. Supports Cognitive Function:

Breakfast is often referred to as "brain food" for good reason. A nutritious breakfast can enhance cognitive function and memory, which is essential for seniors as they face cognitive changes associated with ageing. Consuming complex carbohydrates, such as whole grains, which contain nutrients like anti-oxidants, vitamins and omega-3 fatty acids can provide a steady supply of glucose to the brain, improving concentration and mental alertness.

4. Promotes Emotional Well-being:

Eating a balanced breakfast can have a positive impact on emotional well-being. It can help reduce feelings of anxiety and depression, which are common among seniors, especially those living alone. Breakfast provides an opportunity for seniors to enjoy a comforting and satisfying meal, potentially enhancing their mood and outlook on the day.

5. Social and Emotional benefits:

Breakfast can serve as a social activity for seniors living alone. Sharing a meal with friends or family members can provide a sense of belonging and community, combatting feelings of isolation. Additionally starting the day with a satisfying breakfast can boost mood and emotional wellbeing.

6. Medication Management:

Seniors often have to take multiple medications, some of which require food to be effective or to avoid side effects. Having a nutritious breakfast ensures that seniors can properly manage their medications and maintain their health.

7. Encourages Healthy Eating Habits:

Establishing a routine of having breakfast can set the stage for healthier eating habits throughout the day. Seniors who skip breakfast may be more inclined to make poor food choices later in the day, opting for convenience foods or unhealthy snacks. A nutritious breakfast can help seniors make better food choices and maintain a well balanced diet.

8. Better Physical Health:

A nutritious breakfast is a crucial component of a balanced diet that promotes overall physical health. Fibre-rich foods like whole grains and fruits aid in digestion, prevent constipation, and support gastrointestinal health Adequate protein intake helps maintain muscle mass, bone health, and mobility in seniors.
reducing the risk of hospitalisation, and promoting longevity.

9. Enhanced Immune System:

A well rounded breakfast provides essential vitamins and minerals, such as vitamin C and zinc, that boost the immune system. A robust immune System helps seniors fend off infections and illnesses, reducing the risk of hospitalisation, and promoting longevity.

10. Supports Weight Management:

Eating a healthy breakfast can assist seniors in managing their weight. Maintaining a healthy weight is important for seniors to prevent or manage chronic conditions such as diabetes, heart disease, and arthritis. Contrary to the misconception that skipping meals helps with weight loss, eating a healthy breakfast can actually aid in weight management by preventing overeating and making poor food choices later in the day. A balanced breakfast can also contribute to maintaining a healthy body weight, which is essential for preventing chronic diseases like diabetes and heart disease.

1.3. Maintaining a Healthy Breakfast Routine

Breakfast is often referred to as the most important meal of the day, and for a good reason. It kickstarts your metabolism, provides essential nutrients, and can set the tone for your overall eating habits throughout the day. Maintaining a healthy breakfast routine, especially for seniors living alone, is crucial for overall well-being.

Here are some tips to help you maintain a nutritious breakfast routine:

1. Plan Ahead:

Planning your breakfast the night before can make mornings easier. Decide what you'll have for breakfast and set out the ingredients or prep as much as you can.

2. Keep it Simple:

Breakfast doesn't have to be elaborate. Opt for quick and easy options like yogurt with granola and berries or a smoothie with spinach, banana, and protein powder.

3. Prioritise Protein:

Including a source of protein in your breakfast can help you feel full and satisfied. Consider eggs, Greek yogurt, or cottage cheese.

4. Add Fibre:

Fibre-rich foods like oats, whole-grain bread, and fresh fruits can promote digestive health and keep you feeling full longer.

5. Don't Skip Fruits and Vegetables:

Fresh fruits and vegetables provide essential vitamins, minerals, and antioxidants. Add them to your breakfast whenever possible.

6. Watch Your Portions:

Be mindful of portion sizes, especially if you're preparing a recipe that yields more than one serving. Use measuring cups and utensils to help control portion sizes.

7. Stay Hydrated:

Start your day with a glass of water to rehydrate your body after a night's sleep. You can also enjoy herbal tea or a small glass of 100% fruit juice.

8. Limit Added Sugars:

Be cautious of added sugars in cereals, pastries, and flavoured yogurt. Opt for unsweetened or lightly sweetened options.

9. Read Labels:

When buying packaged foods, read nutrition labels to make informed choices. Look for products with lower sodium and saturated fat content.

10. Listen to Your Body:

Pay attention to your hunger and fullness cues. Eat until you're satisfied but not overly full.

11. Vary Your Breakfasts:

Don't be afraid to try new breakfast recipes and ingredients. Variety ensures you get a range of nutrients.

12. Stay Consistent:

Try to eat breakfast at a consistent time each day. This helps regulate your body's internal clock and can improve your overall eating habits.

13. Seek Professional Advice:

If you have specific dietary concerns or health conditions, consult a healthcare professional or dietitian for personalised breakfast recommendations.

Remember, a healthy breakfast routine sets the foundation for a productive and energetic day. By following these tips and making nutritious choices, you can enjoy the benefits of a balanced breakfast every morning.

1.4. Encouragement for Trying New Recipes

Trying new recipes can be an exciting and rewarding adventure in the kitchen. It's a chance to expand your culinary horizons, discover new flavours, and gain confidence as a home cook.

Here's some encouragement to inspire you to step out of your comfort zone and explore new recipes:

1. Embrace Creativity:

Cooking is a form of art, and each recipe is like a blank canvas waiting for your creative touch. Trying new recipes allows you to experiment with flavours, textures, and presentation.

2. Culinary Exploration:

Think of cooking as a journey of culinary exploration. Just like traveling to new places broadens your horizons, trying new recipes broadens your palate and cooking skills.

3. Expand Your Repertoire:

Trying new recipes adds exciting dishes to your cooking repertoire. It prevents mealtime monotony and ensures you always have a diverse range of meals to enjoy.

4. Cultural Discovery:

Food is a gateway to understanding different cultures. Exploring recipes from around the world can teach you about the history, traditions, and ingredients of various cuisines.

5. Personal Growth:

Learning new cooking techniques and recipes is a form of personal growth. It boosts your confidence and can be a source of pride and accomplishment.

6. Nourish Your Body:

Experimenting with new recipes can lead to discovering healthier and more nutritious options that can benefit your overall well-being.

7. Share Joy:

Cooking and sharing new recipes with friends and family can bring joy and connection. It's a wonderful way to create memorable experiences together.

8. Overcome Fear:

Don't be afraid to make mistakes in the kitchen. Every renowned chef started as a beginner. Mistakes are part of the learning process and can lead to delicious discoveries.

9. Adapt and Modify:

If a recipe seems intimidating, remember that you can adapt and modify it to suit your preferences and skill level. Start with simpler versions and work your way up.

10. Celebrate Successes:

Celebrate your cooking successes, no matter how small they may seem. Each dish you prepare is an achievement, and it's okay to pat yourself on the back.

11. Bond with Food:

Cooking is a way to bond with food on a deeper level. As you engage with ingredients and techniques, you develop a profound appreciation for what you eat.

12. Enjoy the Journey:

Cooking isn't just about the end result; it's about enjoying the journey of creating something delicious. Savour the process, from chopping vegetables to tasting the final product.

13. Inspiration Everywhere:

Inspiration for new recipes can come from cookbooks, websites, TV shows, or even your own cravings. Keep an open mind, and you'll find inspiration everywhere.

14. Stay Curious:

Cultivate a curious attitude in the kitchen. Be open to trying new ingredients and methods, and you'll continually enrich your culinary experience.

Remember that cooking is an evolving skill, and there's always something new to learn. So, don't hesitate to embark on your culinary adventures, and let the joy of trying new recipes fill your kitchen and your plate!

1.5. Cooking Tips and Kitchen Safety for Seniors

Cooking can be a fulfilling and enjoyable activity for seniors, providing not only delicious meals but also a sense of independence. However, it's important to prioritise safety in the kitchen, especially for older adults who may face unique challenges.

This guide offers cooking tips and kitchen safety advice tailored to seniors.

Cooking Tips:

1. Plan Simple and Nutrient-Rich Meals:

Opt for recipes that are easy to prepare and provide essential nutrients. Focus on whole foods like fruits, vegetables, lean proteins, and whole grains.

2. Avoid Over Processed Foods:

60% of the food in a supermarket is likely to fit the definition of over processed, containing additives, flavour enhancers, colouring additives, excess sugar, or sugar substitutes and artificial sweeteners, preservatives and emulsifiers to extend shelf life, or use compounded chocolate which has its valuable cocoa butter replaced with sweeteners, cocoa, and less expensive hard vegetable fat such as coconut oil or palm kernel oil.

3. Kitchen Appliances:

Utilise kitchen appliances like slow cookers, microwave ovens, and toaster ovens to simplify meal preparation. These appliances are often more convenient and safer than traditional stovetop cooking.

4. Prepare Ingredients in Advance:

Prepare ingredients ahead of time to reduce the time and effort required during cooking. Consider using pre-cut vegetables, canned beans, or frozen fruits and vegetables for convenience.

5. Practice Portion Control:

Cooking smaller portions can help prevent food waste and make meal preparation more manageable. Invest in smaller-sized pots and pans if needed.

6. Cook in Batches:

Prepare meals in larger quantities and freeze individual portions for later use. This can save time and effort on busy days.

Kitchen Safety Tips for Seniors

Kitchen safety is crucial for people of all ages, but it becomes even more important as we age, as seniors may be more susceptible to accidents and injuries. Here are some kitchen safety tips tailored specifically for seniors to help them maintain independence and stay safe while cooking:

1. Keep the Kitchen Clean:

Regularly clean countertops, appliances, and utensils to prevent food-borne illnesses. Seniors should be particularly cautious about food safety.

2. Declutter and Organise:

Keep countertops clear of clutter to prevent hazards. Organise your kitchen so that frequently used items are easily accessible without the need to reach or stretch too far.

3. Proper Lighting:

Ensure good lighting in the kitchen to minimise the risk of accidents. Use bright, well-distributed lighting to eliminate shadows. Use task lighting under cabinets if necessary.

4. Non-Slip Flooring:

Install slip resistant flooring in the kitchen to prevent slips and falls. Use non-slip mats or rugs in areas where water may be present such as near the sink or dishwasher.

5. Safe Footwear:

Wear supportive and non-slip footwear with a firm grip in the kitchen to reduce the risk of slipping.

6. Kitchen Tools and Utensils:

Choose utensils and kitchen tools with ergonomic handles that are easy to grip.

Use lightweight cookware to make handling easier.

7. User assistive devices:

Consider using adaptive kitchen tools like jar openers, easy grip utensils, and non-slip mats to make cooking easier and safer.

8. Essential Fire Safety:

Ensure **smoke detectors** are installed in the kitchen and that they are in good working order.

Keep a **fire extinguisher** and **fire blanket** within reach and know how to use them.

Avoid leaving cooking unattended and **use timers** as reminders.

9. Appliance Safety:

Regularly inspect kitchen appliances for any signs of wear, damaged cords or malfunction, and have them serviced if needed.

Consider using appliances with automatic shut-off features.

10. Cooking at Lower Temperatures:

Avoid high-temperature cooking methods, such as frying, as they can lead to hot oil splatters. Opt for baking, broiling, or steaming instead.

11. Timer Usage:

Use timers to remind yourself when food is cooking to prevent overcooking or burning.

12. Hand Hygiene:

Wash your hands before handling food to prevent contamination and food-borne illnesses.

13. Storage Safety:

Store heavy items and frequently used ingredients at waist or eye level to avoid reaching or bending too much. This reduces the risk of strain or injury.

14. Avoid Loose Clothing:

Seniors should avoid wearing loose clothing while cooking to prevent fabric from catching fire or getting entangled in Kitchen equipment.

15. Be Mindful of Hot Surfaces:

Use oven mitts or pot holders when handling hot cookware, and be cautious when opening oven or microwave doors, and saucepan or appliance lids to prevent burns. Silicon sheets are available as effective cover of non-heatproof surfaces, to be able to put hot cooking pans down.

16. Handle Knives Safely:

Use sharp knives for cutting, as dull ones can be more dangerous. Always cut away from your body, and use a cutting board with a non-slip base.

17. Mobility Aids:

If mobility is an issue, consider using a walker or mobility aid with a tray to help carry items safely in the kitchen.

18. Kitchen Helper:

If available, consider having a family member or caregiver assist with meal preparation, especially on occasions when handling hot or heavy items.

19. Emergency Contact:

Ensure that a phone is easily accessible in case of emergencies. Keep a list of emergency contacts, including nearby family members or neighbours, local poison control and healthcare providers, readily available in case of accidents.

20. Medication Awareness:

Be aware of any medications that might affect your alertness or coordination and take them as prescribed.

21. Regular Safety Checks:

Conduct periodic safety checks in the kitchen to identify and address any potential hazards.

22. Food Safety:

Store perishable items in the refrigerator promptly and follow food safety guidelines to prevent food borne illnesses.

23. Stay Alert:

Pay close attention to your cooking. Avoid distractions such as watching television while cooking.

Conclusion:

Cooking can be a fulfilling and empowering activity for seniors, but it is essential to prioritise safety in the kitchen.

By following these cooking and kitchen safety guidelines, older adults can enjoy the pleasures of cooking while minimising the risks associated with meal preparation. Seniors can reduce the risk of accidents and injuries in the kitchen and continue to enjoy the benefits of home-cooked meals safely. Additionally, it's important to adapt these tips to individual needs and abilities, seeking help or making modifications as necessary to maintain kitchen safety. Remember, a safe Kitchen is a happy kitchen.

Chapter 2:

Classic Simple Breakfast Favourites

    2.1. Scrambled Eggs with Spinach

    2.2. Oatmeal with Fresh Berries

    2.3. Whole Grain Toast with Peanut Butter and Banana

    2.4. Overnight Chia Pudding for One

    2.5. Wholegrain Toast with Avocado

2.1. Scrambled Eggs with Spinach

Ingredients:

- 2 large eggs
- 1/2 cup fresh spinach leaves, washed and chopped
- 1 tablespoon butter or olive oil
- Salt and pepper to taste
- Optional: grated cheese (such as cheddar or feta)

Instructions:

Prepare the Ingredients:

Crack the eggs into a bowl and beat them well with a fork or whisk. Wash and chop the spinach leaves.

Heat the Pan:

Place a non-stick skillet over medium-low heat and add the butter or olive oil. Allow it to melt and coat the bottom of the pan evenly.

Sauté the Spinach:

Add the chopped spinach to the pan. Sauté for 1-2 minutes until the spinach begins to wilt and turn bright green.

Add the Eggs:

Pour the beaten eggs over the sautéed spinach in the pan.

Scramble the Eggs:

Use a spatula to gently stir the eggs and spinach mixture continuously as they cook. Keep stirring until the eggs are no longer runny but still slightly moist. This should take about 2-3 minutes.

Season and Serve:

Season the scrambled eggs with salt and pepper to taste.

If you like, you can sprinkle grated cheese over the eggs and let it melt for added flavour.

Plate and Enjoy

Transfer the scrambled eggs with spinach to a plate and serve immediately. They are best enjoyed hot.

Nutritional Benefits:

Eggs are an excellent source of high-quality protein, essential amino acids, and various vitamins and minerals. They contain choline, which is important for brain health, and lutein and zeaxanthin, which promote eye health.

Spinach is rich in vitamins A, C, and K, as well as folate, iron, and calcium. It is also a good source of antioxidants, which help combat free radicals and reduce the risk of chronic diseases.

Butter or Olive Oil: provide healthy fats and add flavor to the dish. Olive oil contains monounsaturated fats, which can have cardiovascular benefits.

Cheese (optional): Cheese adds calcium and protein to the meal. However, it should be consumed in moderation due to its calorie content.

This scrambled eggs with spinach recipe is not only delicious but also packed with essential nutrients. It's a great way to start your day with a healthy and satisfying breakfast.

2.2. Oatmeal with Fresh Berries

Ingredients:

- 1/2 cup old-fashioned rolled oats
- 1 cup milk (or your choice of milk substitute)
- 1/2 cup fresh berries (strawberries, blueberries, raspberries, or a mix)
- 1 tablespoon honey or maple syrup (optional)
- A pinch of salt
- 1/4 teaspoon vanilla extract (optional)
- 1 tablespoon chopped nuts (such as almonds or walnuts) for garnish (optional)

Instructions:

Combine Oats and Milk:

In a saucepan, combine the old-fashioned rolled oats and milk (or milk substitute) over medium heat.

Bring to a Simmer:

Stirring occasionally, bring the mixture to a simmer. Reduce the heat to low to maintain a gentle simmer.

Cook the Oats:

Cook the oats for about 5-7 minutes, or until they reach your desired level of creaminess and thickness. Stir occasionally to prevent sticking.

Add Salt and Optional Ingredients:

Add a pinch of salt and the optional vanilla extract if you like for extra flavor. Stir well.

Sweeten to Taste:

If desired, drizzle honey or maple syrup over the oatmeal to sweeten it. Stir until well combined. Adjust the sweetness to your preference.

Prepare the Berries:

While the oatmeal is cooking, wash and prepare your fresh berries by rinsing them and cutting larger berries into bite-sized pieces if necessary.

Serve:

Once the oatmeal reaches your desired consistency, remove it from the heat and transfer it to a serving bowl.

Top with Berries and Nuts:

Sprinkle the fresh berries over the oatmeal. If you like, garnish with chopped nuts for added texture and flavor.

Enjoy:

Serve your oatmeal with fresh berries immediately while it's warm.

Nutritional Benefits:

Oats are a great source of soluble fiber, which can help lower cholesterol levels and promote heart health. They also provide complex carbohydrates for sustained energy and are rich in vitamins, minerals, and antioxidants.

Berries are packed with antioxidants, including vitamin C and flavonoids, which can help protect cells from damage and reduce the risk of chronic diseases. They are also low in calories and high in fiber, promoting digestive health.

Honey or Maple Syrup (optional): These natural sweeteners provide a touch of sweetness without refined sugars, making this oatmeal a healthier breakfast option.

Nuts (optional) add healthy fats, protein, and crunch to the dish. They are a good source of nutrients like vitamin E, magnesium, and unsaturated fatty acids.

This oatmeal with fresh berries recipe is not only delicious but also nutritious, providing a well-balanced breakfast that will keep you satisfied and energised throughout the morning.

2.3. Whole Grain Toast with Peanut Butter and Banana

Ingredients:

- 2 slices of whole grain bread
- 2 tablespoons of natural peanut butter (unsweetened)
- 1 ripe banana, sliced
- 1 teaspoon honey (optional)
- 1/2 teaspoon cinnamon (optional)
- A pinch of salt (optional)

Instructions:

Toast the bread:

Place the whole grain bread slices in a toaster or on a griddle.

Toast until they are golden brown and crispy.

Spread Peanut Butter:

Once the toast is ready, spread a tablespoon of natural peanut butter on each slice while they are still warm.

If you prefer a sweeter touch, drizzle a teaspoon of honey over the peanut butter.

Add Banana Slices:

Arrange the sliced banana evenly over the peanut butter-covered toast.

Sprinkle with Cinnamon: (Optional)

If desired sprinkle a pinch of cinnamon over the banana slices (optional). Cinnamon pairs wonderfully with the sweetness of the banana and the nuttiness of the peanut butter.

Season with a Pinch of Salt (optional)

If you'd like a touch of saltiness to balance the sweetness, lightly sprinkle a pinch of salt over the top (optional).

Serve and Enjoy:

Your Whole Grain Toast with Peanut Butter and Banana is ready to eat!

Enjoy this nutritious and delicious breakfast or snack option that provides you with a mix of healthy fats, fibre, vitamins and minerals, and antioxidants.

This recipe not only tastes fantastic but also offers a range of nutritional benefits to keep you fuelled and satisfied throughout the day.

Nutritional Benefits:

Whole grain bread is rich in dietary fibre, which aids in digestion and helps regulate blood sugar levels. It's also a good source of complex carbohydrates for sustained energy.

Peanut butter provides healthy fats, protein, and various vitamins and minerals like vitamin E, magnesium, and potassium. It's also a good source of antioxidants and can help reduce the risk of heart disease.

Bananas are a great source of potassium, which is essential for maintaining proper muscle and nerve function. They are also rich in vitamin C and dietary fiber, aiding in digestion and promoting a feeling of fullness.

Honey is a natural sweetener that adds flavor to the dish. It contains antioxidants and has potential anti-inflammatory properties. Choose raw, unprocessed honey for maximum health benefits.

Cinnamon not only adds a delightful flavor but also provides antioxidants and may help lower blood sugar levels and reduce the risk of heart disease.

Salt, a pinch of salt enhances the overall flavor but should be used sparingly to control sodium intake.

2.4. Overnight Chia Pudding for One

Description:

This overnight chia pudding is not only delicious but also packed with nutritional benefits. Chia seeds are a great source of fiber, protein, and healthy fats, while the added fruits and nuts provide vitamins, minerals, and antioxidants. Enjoy this nutritious and easy-to-make breakfast or snack.

Ingredients:

- 1/4 cup chia seeds
- 1 cup almond milk (or any milk of your choice)
- 1 tablespoon honey or maple syrup (optional, for sweetness)
- 1/2 teaspoon vanilla extract
- A pinch of salt
- 1/2 cup fresh berries (e.g., strawberries, blueberries,

raspberries)

- 1/4 cup chopped nuts (e.g., almonds, walnuts, pecans)
- 1/4 cup Greek yogurt (optional, for creaminess)
- Sliced banana or other fruits for topping
- Unsweetened coconut flakes (optional, for garnish)

Instructions:

Mix the Chia Pudding Base:

In a mixing bowl, combine the chia seeds, almond milk, honey or maple syrup (if using), vanilla extract, and a pinch of salt.

Whisk the mixture thoroughly to ensure the chia seeds are well incorporated. This will prevent clumping.

Set and Stir:

Cover the bowl with plastic wrap or a lid and refrigerate it overnight or for at least 4 hours. This allows the chia seeds to absorb the liquid and create a pudding-like consistency.

After about 30 minutes, give the mixture a gentle stir to prevent clumps from forming. Then, stir it again before refrigerating overnight.[2]

Assemble the Pudding:

In the morning or when you're ready to enjoy your pudding, remove it from the refrigerator.

Divide the chia pudding into serving bowls or

glasses.

Add Toppings:

Top the pudding with fresh berries, chopped nuts, and a dollop of Greek yogurt (if desired).

You can also add some sliced banana or other favorite fruits for extra flavor and nutrition.

Garnish and Serve:

Sprinkle with unsweetened coconut flakes or any other desired garnish.

Serve your delicious and nutritious overnight chia pudding immediately, and enjoy!

Nutritional Benefits:

Chia Seeds: Rich in fiber, omega-3 fatty acids, and various vitamins and minerals.

Almond Milk: A low-calorie dairy alternative with vitamin E, calcium, and healthy fats.

Berries: Packed with antioxidants, vitamins, and fiber.

Nuts: Provide healthy fats, protein, and essential minerals like magnesium.

Greek Yogurt: High in protein and probiotics, which are beneficial for gut health.

Honey/Maple Syrup: Optional sweeteners that add a touch of natural sweetness.

Variations:

This overnight chia pudding is not only tasty but also incredibly versatile. Feel free to customize it with your favorite fruits, nuts, and toppings to suit your taste preferences and nutritional needs. Enjoy your wholesome and satisfying breakfast or snack!

2.5. Wholegrain Toast with Avocado for One

Description

This simple and nutritious recipe combines creamy avocado with wholegrain toast for a satisfying breakfast or snack. Avocado is a great source of healthy fats, fiber, and various vitamins and minerals, making it an excellent choice for a quick and healthy meal.

Ingredients:

- 1 ripe avocado
- 1 slice of wholegrain bread
- 1/2 small lemon or lime
- Salt and freshly ground black pepper to taste

- Optional toppings: red pepper flakes, sliced cherry tomatoes, a poached or fried egg, or a sprinkle of your favorite seasoning (e.g., everything bagel seasoning, paprika, or cumin)

Instructions:

Prepare the Avocado:

Cut the ripe avocado in half lengthwise. Remove the pit by gently tapping it with a knife, then twist and remove.

Use a spoon to scoop the flesh of the avocado into a small bowl.

Mash the Avocado:

Using a fork, mash the avocado until you reach your desired level of smoothness. Some people prefer it slightly chunky, while others like it very smooth.

Squeeze the juice from half a lemon or lime over the mashed avocado. The citrus adds a bright flavor and helps prevent the avocado from browning.

Season and Mix:

Season the mashed avocado with a pinch of salt and a few cracks of freshly ground black pepper. Adjust the seasoning to your taste. If you like a little heat, you can add a pinch of red pepper flakes at this stage. Alternatively, you can experiment with other seasonings like smoked paprika or cumin for extra flavor.

Toast the Bread:

Toast the wholegrain bread until it's nicely browned and crisp.

You can use a toaster or a toaster oven.

Assemble the Toast:

Once the toast is ready, spread the mashed avocado evenly onto the warm toast.

Optional Toppings:

Get creative with your toppings. Sliced cherry tomatoes, a poached or fried egg, or additional seasonings can take your avocado toast to the next level. Arrange the toppings on top of the avocado.

Serve and Enjoy:

Serve your wholegrain toast with avocado immediately while it's still warm. It's a perfect breakfast or snack option for one.

Nutritional Benefits:

Avocado is a great source of healthy monounsaturated fats, fiber, vitamins (such as vitamin K, vitamin C, vitamin E, and various B vitamins), and minerals (like potassium and folate).

Wholegrain bread is rich in fiber, which supports digestive health and helps keep you feeling full.

Lemon or lime juice not only adds flavor but also provides a dose of vitamin C.

Optional toppings like tomatoes or eggs can add protein, vitamins, and additional flavors to your toast.

Variations:

This Wholegrain Toast with Avocado is not only delicious but also nutritious and can be customized with optional toppings to suit your taste preferences. Enjoy your tasty and healthy meal!

Chapter 3:

Quick and Easy Breakfasts for Busy Mornings

    3.1. Greek Yogurt Parfait

    3.2. Breakfast Smoothie

    3.3. Cottage Cheese and Pineapple Bowl

    3.4. Mini Quiche

    3.5. Peanut Butter Banana Wrap

    3.6. Classic Pancakes

    3.7. Cinnamon French Toast

3.1. Greek Yogurt Parfait

Ingredients:

- 1 cup of Greek yogurt
- 1/2 cup of granola
- 1 tablespoon of honey
- 1/2 cup of fresh berries (strawberries, blueberries, raspberries, or a mix)
- 1/4 teaspoon of vanilla extract (optional)
- A pinch of cinnamon (optional)

Instructions:

Start by choosing a clear glass or bowl to create beautiful layers in your parfait.

Layer 1: Greek Yogurt

Spoon 1/4 cup of Greek yogurt into the bottom of the glass.

Layer 2: Granola

Sprinkle 2 tablespoons of granola over the yogurt layer.

Layer 3: Berries

Add 1/4 cup of fresh berries on top of the granola.

Layer 4: Repeat the layers with another 1/4 cup of Greek yogurt, 2 tablespoons of granola, and 1/4 cup of berries.

Drizzle with Honey:

Drizzle 1/2 tablespoon of honey over the top layer of berries.

Optional Flavours:

For extra flavour, you can add a splash of vanilla extract or a pinch of cinnamon on top of the honey.

Repeat for More Parfaits:

If you're making more parfaits, repeat the layering process for each glass.

Serve:

Serve your Greek Yogurt Parfait immediately or cover it with plastic wrap and refrigerate for a delightful and healthy breakfast treat.

Nutritional Benefits:

Greek yogurt is a rich source of protein, which helps with muscle health and satiety.

Berries are packed with antioxidants, vitamins, and fiber, promoting heart health and digestion.

Granola provides healthy carbohydrates and fiber for sustained energy throughout the day.

Honey offers natural sweetness and contains antioxidants and antibacterial properties.

Enjoy your delicious and nutritious Greek Yogurt Parfait. It's a fantastic way to start your day with a burst of flavors and essential nutrients.

3.2. Breakfast Smoothie

Ingredients:

- 1 ripe banana
- 1/2 cup of rolled oats
- 1 cup of unsweetened almond milk (or any milk of your choice)
- 1/2 cup of Greek yogurt (or a dairy-free alternative)
- 1 tablespoon of honey (optional for added sweetness)
- 1/2 teaspoon of ground cinnamon
- 1/2 cup of frozen berries (such as strawberries, blueberries, or raspberries)
- 1 tablespoon of chia seeds (optional)
- 1 tablespoon of almond butter (or any nut butter)
- A handful of fresh spinach (optional for added nutrients)

Instructions:

Prepare Ingredients:

Peel the banana and cut it into chunks.

Measure out the rolled oats, almond milk, Greek yogurt, honey, cinnamon, frozen berries, chia seeds, almond butter, and spinach if using.

Blend Smoothie:

Place all the ingredients into a blender.

Blend Until Smooth:

Blend until the mixture is smooth and creamy. You may need to blend for 1-2 minutes, depending on your blender's power.

Taste and Adjust:

Taste the smoothie and adjust sweetness or thickness by adding more honey, almond milk, or yogurt if necessary.

Serve and Enjoy:

Pour the smoothie into a glass and garnish with extra berries or a sprinkle of chia seeds if desired.

Enjoy your nutritious and filling breakfast smoothie that's packed with vitamins, minerals, fiber and protein to kickstart your day.

This breakfast smoothie is not only delicious but also provides a well-rounded mix of nutrients to keep you energised and satisfied throughout the morning. Plus it's a convenient and quick breakfast option for busy mornings.

Nutritional Benefits:

Bananas are a great source of potassium, vitamin C, and dietary fiber. They provide natural sweetness and creaminess to the smoothie.

Rolled Oats are rich in fiber and complex carbohydrates, providing sustained energy and aiding in digestion. They also contain various vitamins and minerals.

Unsweetened almond milk is low in calories and a good source of vitamin E, calcium, and healthy fats, making it a suitable dairy-free option.

Greek yogurt is high in protein, probiotics for gut health, and calcium for bone strength.

Honey adds natural sweetness and provides antioxidants and potential anti-inflammatory properties. It can be omitted for a lower-sugar option.

Cinnamon adds flavor and may help stabilise blood sugar levels.

Berries are rich in antioxidants, vitamins, and dietary fiber. They contribute a burst of flavor and color to the smoothie.

Chia seeds are a great source of omega-3 fatty acids, fiber, and various essential nutrients. They help thicken the smoothie and add a crunchy texture.

Almond butter provides healthy fats, protein, and essential nutrients like vitamin E, magnesium, and potassium.

Spinach is optional but adds extra nutrients, including iron, calcium, and vitamins A and K, without significantly altering the taste.

3.3. Cottage Cheese and Pineapple Bowl

Ingredients:

- 1 cup of low-fat cottage cheese
- 1 cup of fresh pineapple chunks (or canned pineapple in its juice)
- 1/4 cup of chopped fresh mint leaves (optional, for garnish)
- 2 tablespoons of honey (optional, for drizzling)
- 1/4 cup of chopped nuts (such as almonds or walnuts)
- 1/4 teaspoon of ground cinnamon (optional, for sprinkling)

Instructions:

Prepare the Cottage Cheese:

Measure out 1 cup of low-fat cottage cheese and place it in a bowl.

Prepare the Pineapple:

If using fresh pineapple, peel and chop it into bite-sized chunks. If using canned pineapple, drain the juice and use the pineapple chunks.

Assemble the Bowl:

Start by adding the pineapple chunks on top of the cottage cheese.

Garnish with Mint Leaves:

If desired, sprinkle chopped fresh mint leaves over the pineapple and cottage cheese for a burst of freshness.

Drizzle with Honey (Optional):

To add a touch of sweetness, drizzle 2 tablespoons of honey evenly over the ingredients.

Sprinkle with Nuts:

Sprinkle 1/4 cup of chopped nuts (e.g., almonds or walnuts) on top of the bowl for a satisfying crunch and additional nutrients.

Sprinkle with Cinnamon (Optional):

For extra flavor, sprinkle a pinch of ground cinnamon over the top of the bowl.

Serve and Enjoy:

Serve your Cottage Cheese and Pineapple Bowl immediately. Mix the ingredients together if desired, or enjoy them layered.

This delightful bowl is not only a delicious and satisfying snack or breakfast option but also provides a balanced combination of protein, fiber, vitamin, minerals, and antioxidants. It's a great choice for those looking for a healthy and flavorful dish that's quick to prepare.

Nutritional Benefits:

Low-fat cottage cheese is a high-protein dairy product that provides essential amino acids for muscle maintenance and repair. It's also a good source of calcium, aiding in bone health.

Pineapple is rich in vitamin C, which supports the immune system, and contains bromelain, an enzyme that aids in digestion. It's also a source of dietary fiber.

Mint adds a refreshing flavor and contains antioxidants. It may also help with digestion and freshen breath.

Honey serves as a natural sweetener, adding a touch of sweetness to the bowl. It provides antioxidants and potential anti-inflammatory benefits.

Nuts: Chopped nuts offer healthy fats, protein, and various vitamins and minerals, including vitamin E, magnesium, and potassium.

Cinnamon: Cinnamon adds a warm, aromatic flavor and may help stabilize blood sugar levels.

3.4. Mini Quiche for One

Description

This single-serving mini quiche is a delicious and nutritious option for breakfast, brunch, or a light meal. Packed with protein, vitamins, and minerals, it's a satisfying and wholesome dish that's easy to prepare.

Ingredients:

- 1 small egg
- 2 tablespoons milk (you can use dairy or a dairy-free alternative)
- 1 small whole wheat or whole grain pastry shell (store-bought or homemade)
- 2 tablespoons diced vegetables (e.g., bell peppers, spinach, onions, or tomatoes)

- 1 tablespoon grated cheese (e.g., cheddar, Swiss, or feta)
- Salt and pepper to taste
- Fresh herbs (e.g., chopped chives or parsley) for garnish (optional)

Instructions:

Preheat the Oven: Preheat your oven to 350°F (175°C).

Prepare the Pastry Shell:

If using a store-bought pastry shell, you can skip this step. If you're making your own, press the pastry into a small oven-safe ramekin or dish, ensuring it covers the bottom and sides evenly. (You can use the pastry in 4.3. Wholegrain Tortilla Recipe)

Whisk the Egg and Milk:

In a small bowl, whisk together the egg and milk until well combined. Season with a pinch of salt and a dash of black pepper to taste.

Add Vegetables and Cheese:

Sprinkle the diced vegetables and grated cheese evenly over the pastry shell. You can choose your favorite vegetables or use leftovers from your fridge.

Pour the Egg Mixture:

Carefully pour the egg and milk mixture over the vegetables and cheese in the pastry shell. Be sure not to overfill, as the mixture will puff up as it bakes.

Bake the Mini Quiche:

Place the ramekin or dish with the quiche on a baking sheet to catch any spills. Bake in the preheated oven for 20-25 minutes or until the quiche is set and the top is golden brown. The exact cooking time may vary depending on your oven, so keep an eye on it.

Cool and Garnish:

Allow the mini quiche to cool for a few minutes before serving. If desired, garnish with fresh herbs like chopped chives or parsley for extra flavor and presentation.

Serve and Enjoy:

Serve your mini quiche warm as a delightful, single-serving meal.

Nutritional Benefits:

Eggs are an excellent source of high-quality protein and essential nutrients like vitamins (A, B12, D) and minerals (iron, selenium).

Vegetables provide a variety of vitamins, minerals, and dietary fiber, contributing to overall health and well-being.

Fiber: Whole wheat or whole grain pastry shells add fiber, which supports digestive health and helps keep you full.

Cheese adds flavor and provides calcium and protein.

This mini quiche is not only a tasty treat but also a nutritious option to start your day right. Feel free to customize it with your favorite vegetables and cheese to suit your preferences.

3.5. Peanut Butter Banana Wrap

Description

This Peanut Butter Banana Wrap is a quick, delicious, and nutritious option for breakfast, lunch, or a snack. Packed with protein, fiber, and essential nutrients, it's a satisfying and energy-boosting choice.

Ingredients:

- 1 whole wheat or whole grain tortilla (8-10 inches in diameter) (You can use the tortilla in the Wholegrain Tortilla Recipe with 4.1. Breakfast Burrito.)
- 2 tablespoons natural peanut butter (no added sugar or oil)
- 1 ripe banana, peeled and sliced
- 1 tablespoon honey or maple syrup (optional, for added sweetness)
- A sprinkle of ground cinnamon (optional, for extra flavor)

- A small handful of chopped nuts (e.g., almonds or walnuts) for crunch (optional)

Instructions:

- **Prepare the Tortilla:**
- Lay the whole wheat or whole grain tortilla flat on a clean surface or plate.
- **Spread Peanut Butter:**
- Spread the natural peanut butter evenly over the entire surface of the tortilla, leaving a small border around the edges for easier wrapping.
- **Add Sliced Banana:**
- Place the sliced banana evenly on top of the peanut butter-covered tortilla.
- **Drizzle with Sweetener (Optional):**
- If you'd like a touch of added sweetness, drizzle honey or maple syrup over the banana slices.
- **Sprinkle with Cinnamon (Optional):**
- For extra flavor, sprinkle a pinch of ground cinnamon over the banana slices. Cinnamon also adds a warm, comforting aroma.
- **Add Chopped Nuts (Optional):** • If you prefer some crunch in your wrap, sprinkle a small handful of chopped nuts (such as almonds or walnuts) over the banana slices.
- **Wrap It Up:**

- Fold the sides of the tortilla in towards the center, and then roll it up from the bottom to create a wrap.

- **Slice and Serve:**

- Slice the Peanut Butter Banana Wrap in half diagonally to make it easier to eat. You can serve it immediately or wrap it in parchment paper for a convenient on-the-go meal.

Nutritional Benefits:

Peanut butter is a good source of plant-based protein, healthy fats, and essential nutrients like vitamin E, magnesium, and potassium.

Bananas are rich in vitamins (particularly vitamin C and B6), minerals (such as potassium), and dietary fiber.

Whole wheat or whole grain tortillas provide complex carbohydrates and fiber for sustained energy and digestive health.

- **Honey or maple syrup** (if used) adds natural sweetness and a touch of antioxidants.

- **Cinnamon** (if used) not only enhances flavor but also offers potential health benefits, including anti-inflammatory and antioxidant properties.

- **Nuts** (if used) contribute healthy fats, protein, and various vitamins and minerals.

Variations

This Peanut Butter Banana Wrap is a balanced and nutritious option that can satisfy your cravings for something sweet, creamy, and filling.

Customize it to your liking by adding or omitting optional ingredients, and enjoy a tasty and wholesome meal or snack.

3.6. Classic Pancakes for One

Description:

Enjoy a delightful and nutritious breakfast with these classic pancakes for one. These pancakes are light, fluffy, and packed with protein, fiber, and essential nutrients to start your day on the right foot.

Ingredients:

- 1/2 cup whole wheat flour (or a mix of whole wheat and all-purpose flour)
- 1 tablespoon sugar or a natural sweetener of your choice (e.g., honey, maple syrup, or agave nectar)
- 1/2 teaspoon baking powder
- 1/4 teaspoon baking soda
- A pinch of salt

- 1/2 cup buttermilk (or a mixture of milk and yogurt)
- 1 small egg
- 1/2 teaspoon pure vanilla extract
- Cooking spray or a small amount of butter or oil for cooking
- Fresh berries, sliced banana, or a sprinkle of nuts for topping (optional)

Instructions:

Mix Dry Ingredients:

In a mixing bowl, combine the whole wheat flour, sugar (or sweetener), baking powder, baking soda, and a pinch of salt. Stir to combine the dry ingredients evenly.

Whisk Wet Ingredients:

In a separate bowl, whisk together the buttermilk, egg, and vanilla extract until well blended.

Combine Wet and Dry Mixtures:

Pour the wet mixture into the bowl with the dry ingredients. Stir until just combined. It's okay if there are a few lumps; over-mixing can make the pancakes less fluffy.

Preheat Griddle or Pan:

Preheat a non-stick griddle or frying pan over medium heat. If using a regular pan, lightly grease it with cooking spray, butter, or a small amount of oil.

Cook Pancakes:

Pour 1/4 cup of the pancake batter onto the hot griddle or pan for each pancake. Cook until bubbles form on the surface and the edges start to look set, usually about 2-3 minutes.

Flip the pancakes with a spatula and cook for an additional 1-2 minutes on the other side, or until they're golden brown and cooked through.

Serve Warm:

Transfer the pancakes to a plate. If desired, top them with fresh berries, sliced banana, or a sprinkle of nuts for added nutrition and flavor.

Enjoy:

Serve your classic pancakes warm with a drizzle of maple syrup, a dollop of Greek yogurt, or a sprinkle of cinnamon, as desired.

Nutritional Benefits:

Whole wheat flour adds dietary fiber, vitamins (such as B vitamins), and minerals (including magnesium and iron) to the pancakes.

Eggs provide high-quality protein and essential nutrients like choline and vitamin D.

Buttermilk or a milk-yogurt mixture adds calcium and protein.

Fresh berries, banana, or nuts provide vitamins, minerals, antioxidants, and dietary fiber.

Variation:

A traditional way to eat pancakes is to make the pancakes larger, and to roll them, adding the toppings over the length of the roll. You can optionally sprinkle sugar, or drizzle 62honey, and squeeze lemon juice along the rolled up pancake.

These classic pancakes are not only delicious but also offer a balanced mix of carbohydrates, protein, and fiber to keep you satisfied and energized throughout the morning. Enjoy your nutritious breakfast!

3.7. Cinnamon French Toast

Description

This French toast recipe is not only delicious but also offers nutrition benefits, especially from the addition of cinnamon. Cinnamon is known for its potential health benefits, including improved blood sugar control and antioxidant properties.

Ingredients:

- 2 slices of whole-grain bread (gluten-free if needed)
- 2 large eggs
- 1/4 cup unsweetened almond milk (or any milk of your choice)
- 1/2 teaspoon ground cinnamon
- 1/2 teaspoon pure vanilla extract
- Cooking spray or a small amount of butter for the pan

- Fresh berries or sliced banana for topping (optional)
- Pure maple syrup for drizzling (optional)

Instructions:

Prepare the Batter:

In a shallow bowl, whisk together the eggs, almond milk, ground cinnamon, and pure vanilla extract until well combined.

Dip the Bread:

Heat a non-stick skillet or griddle over medium heat and lightly grease it with cooking spray or a small amount of butter.

Dip each slice of whole-grain bread into the egg mixture, making sure both sides are well coated but not soaked.

Cook the French Toast:

Place the dipped bread slices onto the hot skillet. Cook for about 2-3 minutes on each side, or until they are golden brown and crispy.

Serve:

Transfer the cinnamon French toast to a plate. Top with fresh berries or sliced banana if desired.

Drizzle with pure maple syrup for a touch of sweetness if you like.

These cinnamon French toast slices are not only delicious but also provide a good source of protein from the eggs and whole grains from the bread. The cinnamon adds flavor and potential health benefits.

Nutrition Benefits:

Whole-Grain Bread: Using whole-grain bread provides fiber, vitamins, and minerals that are not found in refined white bread. It also helps maintain steady blood sugar levels.

Eggs: Eggs are a great source of high-quality protein, essential vitamins, and minerals, including vitamin B12, vitamin D, and choline.

Cinnamon: Cinnamon has antioxidant properties and may help improve insulin sensitivity, making it a good choice for those concerned about blood sugar control.

Enjoy your cinnamon French toast as a satisfying and nutritious breakfast option. It's a delicious way to start your day with a boost of flavor and potential health benefits.

Chapter 4:

Hearty Traditional Breakfast Favorites

    4.1. Breakfast Burrito

    4.2. Wholegrain Tortilla Recipe

    4.3. Vegetable Frittata for One

    4.4. Creamy Oat Porridge with Nuts and Honey

    4.5 Breakfast Casserole with Wholegrain Bread and Turkey

    4.6. Birthday Pancake Stack

4.1. Breakfast Burrito

Ingredients:

(For 4 Burrito servings)

For the Burrito Filling:

- 4 large eggs (quantity and size optional)
- 1/4 cup diced bell peppers (any colour)
- 1/4 cup diced onions
- 1/4 cup diced tomatoes
- 1/4 cup diced cooked ham or turkey bacon (optional)
- 1/4 cup shredded cheddar cheese (reduced-fat if preferred)
- Salt and pepper to taste
- Cooking oil or non-stick cooking spray

For Assembling:

- 4 whole wheat or whole grain tortillas
- Salsa, hot sauce, or avocado (optional, for serving)
- Fresh cilantro or parsley (optional, for garnish)

Instructions:

Prepare the Filling

In a bowl, whisk the eggs and season with salt and pepper.

Heat a non-stick skillet over medium-high heat, add a little cooking oil or non-stick cooking spray, and sauté the diced onions and bell peppers until they become slightly tender (about 2-3 minutes).

Add the diced tomatoes and ham or turkey bacon (if using) to the skillet and cook for an additional 2 minutes.

Cook the Eggs:

Pour the whisked eggs into the skillet with the vegetables and cook, stirring gently, until the eggs are scrambled and fully cooked.

Add Cheese:

Sprinkle the shredded cheddar cheese over the scrambled eggs and let it melt.

Warm Tortillas:

While the cheese is melting, warm the tortillas in a dry skillet or microwave for about 10 seconds to make them pliable.

Assemble the Burritos:

Divide the scrambled egg mixture evenly among the tortillas.

Fold and Roll:

Fold in the sides of each tortilla and then roll it up tightly, creating a burrito.

Serve:

Optionally, serve your breakfast burrito with salsa, hot sauce, avocado slices, or fresh cilantro or parsley for extra flavor.

Nutritional Benefits:

Eggs are rich in high-quality protein and provide essential nutrients like choline and B vitamins. They can support muscle growth and brain function.

Bell peppers are low in calories and high in vitamin C, vitamin A, and fiber, promoting healthy skin, immune function, and digestion.

Onions add flavor and are a good source of antioxidants and vitamins, including vitamin C and vitamin B6.

Tomatoes provide vitamin C, potassium, and lycopene, an antioxidant that may reduce the risk of chronic diseases.

Ham or Turkey Bacon (optional): Lean proteins like turkey bacon or ham (optional) contribute to muscle maintenance and repair.

Cheddar cheese offers calcium and protein, which are essential for bone health and muscle function.

Whole wheat or whole grain tortillas provide dietary fiber, complex carbohydrates, and essential nutrients like magnesium and iron.

4.2. Wholegrain Tortilla Recipe

Description

Super soft flat bread for any filling.

Ingredients:

- Sift 350 grams of flour (2 1/4 cups).
- Add 1 teaspoon salt (5 grams).
- 2 teaspoons vegetable oil (30 milliliters).
- 200 milliliters boiling water (4/5 cup).

Instructions:

Add Ingredients to bowl and stir with a spoon.

Knead by hand for 2 minutes.

The dough is very soft and elastic.

Cover the dough and let it rest for 15 minutes.

Sprinkle the table with flour and roll out the dough into a roll. *

Divide the dough into 12 pieces.

Make dough balls.

Cover the dough while you cook so it doesn't dry out.

Roll out the dough thinly.

Make a round shape to fit the diameter of your pan (mine is 26 centimeter / 10 inches).

Make a medium heat and heat the pan.

Cook 40 seconds on one side, then flip.

While you are preparing this flat bread, roll out the next one.

Cook for a maximum of 2 minutes, the main thing is not to over-dry.

Brush the hot bread immediately with hot water.

Grease the edges especially well on both sides.

Cover with cling film.

The process of making bread is very fast.

Repeat the same steps for the rest of the raw tortillas.

Make sure the bread doesn't burn.

Brush with hot water each time.

When the last bread is done, cover with cling film and let the bread rest covered for 30 minutes.

After that, the bread will be very soft and will not break.

Use it as a wrap for any topping!

4.3. Vegetable Frittata for One

Description

This vegetable frittata for one is a quick and nutritious meal that's perfect for a solo breakfast, brunch, or even a light dinner. Packed with fresh vegetables and protein, it provides a balanced mix of vitamins, minerals, and energy to fuel your day. Feel free to customize the veggies to your liking.

Ingredients:

- 1/2 tablespoon olive oil
- 1/4 cup diced onion
- 1/4 cup diced bell pepper (any colour)
- 1/4 cup diced zucchini
- 1/4 cup cherry tomatoes, halved
- 2 large eggs
- 2 tablespoons milk (any type)

-
- Salt and pepper to taste
- 1/4 cup grated cheese (cheddar, mozzarella, or your favourite)

Fresh herbs (such as parsley or chives) for garnish (optional)

Instructions:

Preheat your oven to 350°F (175°C).

In a non-stick oven-safe skillet (about 8 inches in diameter), heat the olive oil over medium heat, on top of the stove.

Add the diced onion and bell pepper to the skillet. Sauté for about 2-3 minutes, or until they begin to soften.

Add the diced zucchini and cherry tomatoes to the skillet. Continue to sauté for another 2-3 minutes until the vegetables are slightly tender.

Season with a pinch of salt and pepper.

In a bowl, whisk together the eggs and milk until well combined.

Season the egg mixture with a pinch of salt and pepper to taste.

Pour the egg mixture evenly over the sautéed vegetables in the skillet.

Sprinkle the grated cheese evenly over the top of the frittata. This adds a creamy and delicious touch while also boosting the protein content.

Place the skillet in the preheated oven and bake for about 15-20 minutes or until the frittata is set in the center and the top is golden brown. You can check for doneness by inserting a knife into the centre – it should come out clean.

Carefully remove the skillet from the oven using oven mitts, as the handle will be hot. Let it cool for a minute or two before slicing.

Garnish with fresh herbs if desired.

Nutritional Benefits:

Eggs and Cheese: Protein from eggs and cheese helps to keep you full and provides essential amino acids.

Vegetables: Vitamins and minerals from the variety of vegetables, including vitamin C from bell peppers and vitamin K from zucchini.

Fiber from the vegetables aids digestion and provides a sense of fullness.

Olive Oil: Healthy fats from olive oil contribute to heart health.

Cheese: Calcium and protein from cheese support bone and muscle health.

Variations:

You can also pair your Vegetable Frittata with a side salad or some whole-grain toast.

4.4. Creamy Oat Porridge with Nuts and Honey

Ingredients:

- 1/2 cup rolled oats
- 1 cup milk (any type: dairy, almond, soy, etc.)
- 1/4 teaspoon ground cinnamon (optional)
- Pinch of salt (optional)
- 1-2 tablespoons honey (adjust to taste)
- 2 tablespoons chopped mixed nuts (e.g., almonds, walnuts, or pecans)
- Fresh berries or sliced banana (optional, for topping)
- Extra honey for drizzling (optional)

Instructions:

Combine the ingredients in a medium saucepan, rolled oats, milk, ground cinnamon (if using), and a pinch of salt. Stir well to combine.

Place the saucepan over medium-high heat and bring the mixture to a gentle boil, stirring occasionally to prevent sticking. This should take about 5-7 minutes.

Reduce the heat once the mixture begins to boil, to low and let it simmer. Continue to cook for an additional 3-5 minutes, or until the oats have absorbed most of the liquid and the porridge reaches your desired creamy consistency.

Be sure to stir frequently to avoid lumps and sticking to the bottom of the pan.

Remove the saucepan from the heat and stir in 1-2 tablespoons of honey, adjusting the sweetness to your preference. Mix until the honey is fully incorporated into the porridge.

Lightly toast the chopped nuts in a small skillet, over medium-low heat for 2-3 minutes, or until they become fragrant and slightly golden. Keep an eye on them, as they can quickly burn.

Pour the creamy oat porridge into a serving bowl. Top it with the toasted nuts and fresh berries or sliced banana, if desired.

Drizzle a bit of extra honey over the top for added sweetness, if you like.

Serve your creamy oat porridge hot and enjoy!

Variations:

Feel free to use additional toppings such as chia seeds, shredded coconut, or a dollop of Greek yogurt for extra creaminess.

Nutritional Benefits:

Oats are a great source of fiber, keeping you feeling full and aiding in digestion.

Nuts provide healthy fats, protein, and essential nutrients like vitamin E and magnesium.

Honey adds natural sweetness along with antioxidants and potential allergy relief.

Milk provides calcium and vitamin D for strong bones.

This creamy oat porridge is not only delicious, but also a wholesome way to start your day. It is easily adaptable to your preferences, making it a versatile and satisfying breakfast option.

4.5. Breakfast Casserole with Wholegrain Bread and Turkey

Description

This single-serve holiday breakfast casserole is packed with flavor, using whole-grain bread and lean turkey or chicken for added nutritional benefits. It's a hearty and satisfying breakfast perfect for a festive occasion or any time you want a special morning treat.

Ingredients:

- 1 slice of whole-grain bread, cubed (about 1 cup of cubes)
- 1/4 cup cooked turkey or chicken breast, diced
- 1/4 cup shredded low-fat cheese (such as cheddar or mozzarella)
- 1/4 cup diced bell peppers (any color)
- 2 tablespoons diced red onion

- 1 small garlic clove, minced
- 2 large eggs
- 1/4 cup unsweetened almond milk (or any milk of your choice)
- 1/4 teaspoon dried thyme
- 1/4 teaspoon dried rosemary
- Salt and pepper to taste
- Fresh parsley or chives for garnish (optional)

Instructions:

Prepare the Bread and Meat:

Preheat your oven to 350°F (175°C).

Cube the whole-grain bread and place it in a single-serving oven-safe dish or ramekin.

Add Turkey or Chicken:

Sprinkle the diced turkey or chicken over the bread cubes.

Add Veggies:

Scatter the diced bell peppers and red onion over the turkey or chicken.

Sprinkle Cheese:

Sprinkle the shredded low-fat cheese evenly over the vegetables.

Whisk Eggs and Milk:

In a small bowl, whisk together the eggs, almond milk, minced garlic, dried thyme, dried rosemary, salt, and pepper.

Pour Over Mixture:

Pour the egg mixture over the bread, turkey, veggies, and cheese. Make sure it soaks into the bread.

Bake:

Place the dish in the preheated oven and bake for 20-25 minutes, or until the casserole is puffy, golden brown, and set in the center.

Garnish and Serve:

Remove the casserole from the oven and let it cool for a minute.

Garnish with fresh parsley or chives, if desired.

Serve your delicious holiday breakfast casserole while it's warm.

Nutritional Benefits:

Whole-Grain Bread: Provides fiber and complex carbohydrates for sustained energy.

Turkey or Chicken: Lean protein source, rich in vitamins and minerals like B vitamins, selenium, and zinc.

Low-Fat Cheese: Adds calcium and protein without excess saturated fat.

Bell Peppers: Provide vitamin C and antioxidants.

Eggs: Excellent source of protein, vitamins, and minerals like vitamin B12, vitamin D, and choline.

This single-serve holiday breakfast casserole not only tastes great but also offers a balance of nutrients to keep you satisfied and energized throughout the day. Enjoy the warmth and flavor of the holiday season in every bite!

4.6. Birthday Pancake stack

Description

This birthday pancake stack is a delightful and nutritious way to celebrate a special occasion or simply treat yourself. These pancakes are made with whole grains, yogurt, and fruit, providing a balance of flavors and essential nutrients.

Ingredients:

- 1/2 cup whole wheat flour
- 1/4 cup rolled oats
- 1/2 teaspoon baking powder
- 1/4 teaspoon baking soda
- 1/4 teaspoon ground cinnamon
- Pinch of salt

- 1/2 cup plain Greek yogurt (or your preferred yogurt)
- 1/4 cup unsweetened applesauce
- 1 large egg
- 1/2 teaspoon pure vanilla extract
- 1/4 cup fresh mixed berries (strawberries, blueberries, raspberries)
- 1 tablespoon honey or pure maple syrup (for drizzling)
- Whipped cream (optional, for garnish)
- Sprinkles (optional, for decoration)

Instructions:

Prepare the Dry Ingredients:

In a mixing bowl, combine the whole wheat flour, rolled oats, baking powder, baking soda, ground cinnamon, and a pinch of salt. Mix well.

Create the Wet Mixture:

In another bowl, whisk together the Greek yogurt, unsweetened applesauce, egg, and vanilla extract until smooth.

Combine Dry and Wet Ingredients:

Pour the wet mixture into the dry ingredients and stir until just combined. Be careful not to overmix; a few lumps are okay.

Cook the Pancakes:

Heat a non-stick skillet or griddle over medium heat and lightly grease it with cooking spray or a small amount of butter.

Pour 1/4 cup portions of the pancake batter onto the skillet to form pancakes. Cook until bubbles form on the surface and the edges look set, about 2-3 minutes.

Flip and Cook the Other Side:

Gently flip the pancakes and cook for an additional 1-2 minutes, or until they are golden brown and cooked through.

Stack the Pancakes:

As the pancakes finish cooking, stack them on a serving plate.

Add Toppings:

Top the stack of pancakes with fresh mixed berries, a drizzle of honey or pure maple syrup, and a dollop of whipped cream if desired.

Decorate:

Sprinkle some colorful sprinkles on top to make it extra festive.

Serve:

Serve your birthday pancake stack while it's warm and enjoy!

Nutritional Benefits:

Whole Wheat Flour: Provides fiber, vitamins, and minerals compared to refined flour.

Rolled Oats: Rich in fiber and essential nutrients like manganese and phosphorus.

Greek Yogurt: High in protein, calcium, and probiotics for gut health.

Fresh Berries: A great source of antioxidants, vitamins, and fiber.

Honey or Maple Syrup: Natural sweeteners with a lower glycemic index compared to refined sugar.

Description:

This birthday pancake stack offers a balanced combination of carbohydrates, protein, and fiber, making it a delicious and nutritious way to celebrate your special day or any breakfast occasion. Enjoy!

Chapter 5:

Special Occasion Breakfasts

5.1. Blueberry Pancakes with Blueberry Compote

5.2. Eggs Benedict

5.3. English Muffin Recipe

5.4. Smoked Salmon Bagel

5.1. Blueberry Pancakes with Blueberry Compote

Ingredients:

For the Pancakes:

- 1/2 cup all-purpose flour (or wholewheat flour if you prefer)
- 1/2 teaspoon baking powder
- 1/4 teaspoon baking soda
- 1/4 teaspoon salt
- 1 tablespoon honey or maple syrup

- 1/2 cup low-fat or almond milk
- 1/4 cup plain Greek yogurt (for added protein and creaminess)
- 1/2 teaspoon pure vanilla extract
- 1 egg
- Cooking spray or a small amount of olive oil or butter for greasing the pan

For the Blueberry Compote:

- 1/2 cup fresh or frozen blueberries
- 1 tablespoon water
- 1 tablespoon sugar (or a healthier alternative like stevia or honey)
- 1/2 teaspoon lemon zest (optional)

Instructions:

For the Blueberry Compote:

In a small saucepan, combine the blueberries, water, sugar (or substitute), and lemon zest (if using).

Heat the mixture over medium-low heat, stirring occasionally, until the blueberries start to break down and the mixture thickens (usually about 10 minutes).

Remove from heat and let it cool while you prepare the pancakes.

For the Pancakes:

In a mixing bowl, whisk together the flour, baking powder, baking soda, salt, and sugar.

In another bowl, combine the milk, Greek yogurt, vanilla extract, and egg. Mix until well blended.

Pour the wet ingredients into the dry ingredients and stir until just combined. Be careful not to over-mix; it's okay if there are a few lumps.

Heat a non-stick skillet or griddle over medium heat and lightly grease it with cooking spray or a small amount of butter.

For each pancake, pour about 1/4 cup of the batter onto the hot skillet. You can make smaller or larger pancakes depending on your preference.

Cook the pancakes until you see bubbles forming on the surface and the edges start to set, usually about 2-3 minutes.

Flip the pancakes and cook for an additional 1-2 minutes or until they are golden brown and cooked through.

Repeat with the remaining batter.

To Serve:

Place the cooked pancakes on a plate.

Spoon the warm blueberry compote over the pancakes.

Drizzle a little extra honey or maple syrup on top for added sweetness if desired.

Nutrition Benefits:

These blueberry pancakes with blueberry compote offer a nutritious and delicious meal for one person:

Blueberries are rich in antioxidants and vitamins, especially vitamin C and vitamin K. They are also low in calories and high in fiber.

Greek yogurt adds protein and creaminess to the pancake batter, making them more filling.

Whole eggs provide protein and essential nutrients like choline and vitamins B12 and D.

Low-fat or almond milk is a source of calcium and vitamin D, which are essential for bone health.

Honey or maple syrup (used in moderation) provides a natural sweetener with potential health benefits when compared to refined sugar.

The compote made from blueberries is an extra source of antioxidants, fiber, and natural sweetness without added sugar.

The lemon zest adds a refreshing citrus flavor and provides a touch of vitamin C.

5.2. Eggs Benedict for One

Ingredients:

For the Hollandaise Sauce:

- 1 large egg yolk
- 1/2 teaspoon Dijon mustard
- 1/2 teaspoon lemon juice
- Pinch of salt
- Pinch of cayenne pepper (optional)
- 2 tablespoons unsalted butter, melted

For the Eggs Benedict:

- 1 whole wheat English muffin, split and toasted
- 1 slice Canadian bacon or ham (approximately 1 ounce)
- 1 large egg, or 2 small eggs
- Fresh chives or parsley, for garnish (optional)
- Salt and pepper, to taste

Instructions:

For the Hollandaise Sauce:

In a small bowl, whisk together the egg yolk, Dijon mustard, lemon juice, salt, and cayenne pepper (if using). **Slowly drizzle** in the melted butter while continuing to whisk vigorously until the sauce thickens. This should take about 2-3 minutes. Heat in a small saucepan.

Once the sauce has thickened, remove it from the heat and keep it warm.

For the Eggs Benedict:

Heat the water. Fill a small saucepan with water until it's about two-thirds full. Add a pinch of salt and bring the water to a gentle simmer over medium heat.

While the water is heating, toast the whole wheat English muffin halves.

In a separate skillet, lightly brown the Canadian bacon or ham slice on both sides. Remove from the skillet and keep warm.

Once the water in the saucepan is simmering, create a gentle whirlpool by stirring the water in one direction. Crack the egg into a small bowl and gently slide it into the center of the whirlpool. Cook for about 3-4 minutes for a soft, runny yolk or longer for a firmer yolk.

Carefully remove the poached egg from the water using a slotted spoon and place it on a paper towel to drain any excess water.

Assemble your Eggs Benedict: Place the toasted English muffin halves on a plate, top each half with the Canadian bacon or ham slice, and then add the poached egg on top.

Spoon the Hollandaise sauce over the eggs.

Garnish with chopped fresh chives or parsley (if desired), and season with a pinch of salt and pepper.

Nutritional Benefits:

This single-serving Eggs Benedict recipe provides several nutritional benefits:

Protein: Eggs are an excellent source of high-quality protein.

Whole Wheat English Muffin: Whole wheat provides fiber, vitamins, and minerals, adding nutritional value compared to white bread.

Canadian Bacon or Ham: Provides lean protein and essential nutrients.

Hollandaise Sauce: Contains protein from the egg yolk and healthy fats from the butter.

Eggs: Rich in essential vitamins and minerals, including vitamin D, B vitamins, and choline.

Dijon Mustard and Lemon Juice: Add flavor and a small amount of vitamin C.

Cayenne Pepper: If used, provides a hint of spice and potential metabolism-boosting benefits.

Fresh Herbs (Chives or Parsley): Add flavor and small amounts of vitamins and antioxidants.

5.3. English Muffin Recipe

Ingredients:

- 450g (about 3 cups) bread flour

- 1 packet (7g or 2 1/4 tsp) active dry yeast

- 1 tablespoon sugar

- 1 teaspoon salt

- 1 cup warm milk (around 110°F/43°C)

- 2 tablespoons unsalted butter, melted

- 1 egg, lightly beaten

- Cornmeal, for dusting

Instructions:

Prepare the Dough:

- In a large bowl, mix together the flour, yeast, sugar, and salt.
- In a separate bowl, combine the warm milk, melted butter, and beaten egg.
- Gradually add the wet ingredients to the dry ingredients, mixing until a soft dough forms. You might not need all the liquid, so add gradually until the dough is pliable and slightly tacky, not wet.

Knead the Dough:

- Turn the dough out onto a floured surface and knead for about 10 minutes until smooth and elastic.
- Place the dough in a lightly oiled bowl, cover with plastic wrap or a damp cloth, and let rise in a warm place until doubled in size, about 1 hour.

Shape the Muffins:

- Punch down the risen dough and turn it out onto a lightly floured surface.
- Roll out to about 1/2 inch thickness. Using a round cutter or a wide-mouthed glass, cut out rounds from the dough.

- Sprinkle cornmeal on a parchment-lined baking sheet, place the dough rounds on the sheet, and sprinkle more cornmeal on top of the rounds.

- Cover loosely with plastic wrap and let them rise for another 30 minutes.

Cook the Muffins:

- Heat a skillet or griddle over medium-low heat. Once hot, cook the muffins (without overcrowding) for about 5-7 minutes per side until they are golden brown and cooked through.

Cool and Serve

- Transfer the cooked muffins to a wire rack to cool. They can be split open with a fork and toasted before serving.

Enjoy your homemade English muffins with butter, jam, or use them as the base for a delicious eggs Benedict!

Variation:

You can use wholemeal flour instead of bread flour to make English muffins for a heartier and more nutritious version. Keep in mind that wholemeal flour absorbs more liquid than white flour, so you might need to adjust the amount of milk slightly to get the right dough consistency. The texture will also be denser, and the muffins might not rise as much as with bread flour. If you like, you can mix wholemeal and bread flour to strike a balance between texture and nutritional content.

5.4. Smoked Salmon Bagel for One

Ingredients:

- 1 bagel (whole wheat, plain, or your choice)
- 2 oz smoked salmon
- 2 tablespoons cream cheese (regular or low-fat)
- 1 tablespoon capers, drained
- 1-2 thin slices of red onion
- 1-2 slices of tomato
- Fresh dill sprigs, for garnish (optional)
- Lemon wedges, for serving (optional)
- Salt and black pepper, to taste

Instructions:

Slice and Toast the Bagel:

Slice the bagel in half:

Toast it in a toaster or under a broiler until it's lightly crispy but not overly browned.

Spread Cream Cheese:

While the bagel is still warm, spread the cream cheese on each half. Adjust the amount to your preference.

Layer with Smoked Salmon:

Lay the smoked salmon slices evenly on top of the cream cheese, covering the entire surface of the bagel.

Add Tomato and Onion:

Place the tomato slices on top of the salmon.

Add the thinly sliced red onion on top.

Sprinkle with Capers:

Scatter the capers evenly over the cream cheese and bagel.

Season and Garnish:

Season the open-faced bagel sandwich with a pinch of salt and a sprinkle of black pepper.

Garnish with fresh dill sprigs if you like. Dill pairs beautifully with smoked salmon.

Serve and Enjoy:

Serve your smoked salmon bagel open-faced, or you can place the other half of the bagel on top to make it a sandwich. Optionally, serve with lemon wedges on the side for a citrusy touch.

Nutritional Benefits:

Smoked Salmon: Rich in omega-3 fatty acids, high-quality protein, and essential vitamins and minerals like vitamin D, B vitamins, and selenium.

Bagel: Provides carbohydrates for energy, and if you choose a whole wheat bagel, it adds dietary fiber and more nutrients compared to white bagels.

Cream Cheese: While it's indulgent, it contributes some protein and calcium.

Tomato: Offers vitamins C and A, as well as lycopene, an antioxidant.

Red Onion: Contains antioxidants and a small amount of fiber.

Capers: Provide a burst of flavor and a bit of fiber.

Dill: If you choose to garnish with dill, it adds a refreshing herb flavor and may have mild antioxidant properties.

Lemon Wedges: If used, they add vitamin C and a bright, citrusy flavor.

Enjoy your home made smoked salmon bagel as a satisfying and nutritious breakfast, brunch or snack!

Chapter 6:

Breakfasts for Seniors with Dietary Considerations

6.1. Nutrient-Packed Low Sugar Breakfast Bowl

6.2. Low-Sodium Veggie and Egg Scramble

6.3. Gluten-Free Banana Oat Pancakes

Note:

Know your own dietary considerations, and ask guests if they have dietary preferences or limitations. Offer to show them the ingredient list for any meals if there are any foods that they must avoid, or can not eat.

6.1. Nutrient-Packed Low Sugar Breakfast Bowl

Description:

Start your day right with this delicious and nutritious low-sugar breakfast bowl that's packed with dietary benefits. It's a perfect choice for one person and providers essential nutrients to keep you energized throughout the morning.

Ingredients:

- 1/2 cup rolled oats (gluten-free if needed)
- 1 cup unsweetened almond milk (or your preferred milk)
- 1/2 ripe banana, sliced
- 1/4 cup fresh mixed berries (e.g., strawberries, blueberries, raspberries)
- 1 tablespoon chia seeds

- 1 tablespoon unsweetened natural almond butter
- 1/2 teaspoon ground cinnamon
- A handful of chopped nuts (e.g., almonds, walnuts, or pecans)
- A drizzle of honey or maple syrup (optional)
- A pinch of salt (optional)

Instructions:

Combine Rolled Oats and Milk:

In a microwave-safe bowl or a small saucepan, combine the rolled oats and almond milk (or your preferred milk). If you'd like a creamier consistency, you can add a pinch of salt at this stage. Stir well.

Cook Oats:

If using a microwave, microwave the oatmeal on high for 2-3 minutes, stopping to stir every minute until the oats are tender and the mixture thickens. If using a saucepan, cook over medium heat, stirring constantly, until the oats are cooked to your desired consistency.

Prepare Toppings:

While the oats are cooking, prepare your toppings.
Slice the ripe banana and wash the mixed berries.
In a small bowl, mix the chia seeds with a couple of tablespoons of water. Let them sit for a few minutes until they form a gel-like consistency. Stir well to ensure there are no clumps.

Assemble Your Bowl:

Once the oats are cooked, transfer them to a serving bowl.

Top the oatmeal with the sliced banana, mixed berries, and a dollop of almond butter.

Sprinkle ground cinnamon evenly over the top.

Drizzle a touch of honey or maple syrup if you desire extra sweetness. Remember, the ripe banana and berries provide natural sweetness, so adjust according to your preference.

Add Chia Seeds and Nuts:

Spoon the chia seed mixture over your bowl. This adds extra fiber and omega-3 fatty acids.

Finish by sprinkling chopped nuts of your choice for added crunch and healthy fats.

Nutritional Benefits:

This breakfast is **low in added sugars**, making it suitable for individuals aiming to reduce their sugar intake.

It's rich in dietary fiber from **oats, chia seeds, and berries**, promoting digestive health and helping you feel full for longer.

The **banana** adds potassium and natural sweetness, while berries offer antioxidants and vitamins.

Almond butter and nuts provide healthy fats and protein to keep you satisfied and provide long-lasting energy.

Cinnamon not only adds flavor but may also help regulate blood sugar levels.

Optional **honey** or **maple syrup** can be used sparingly for added sweetness without spiking blood sugar.

6.2. Low-Sodium Veggie and Egg Scramble

Description:

This low-sodium breakfast recipe is not only delicious but also packed with dietary benefits. It's high in protein and fiber, making it a nutritious way to start your day. Plus, it's easy to prepare for one person.

Ingredients:

- 2 large eggs

- 1/4 cup diced bell peppers (any color)
- 1/4 cup diced tomatoes
- 1/4 cup diced onions
- 1/4 cup chopped spinach or kale
- 1/2 teaspoon olive oil
- Salt-free seasoning blend (to taste)
- Freshly ground black pepper (to taste)
- 1/4 avocado (optional, for garnish)
- Fresh herbs like parsley or chives (optional, for garnish)

Instructions:

Prepare the Veggies:

Heat a non-stick skillet over medium heat and add the olive oil.

Add the diced onions and bell peppers. Sauté for 2-3 minutes until they start to soften.

Add Tomatoes and Greens:

Stir in the diced tomatoes and chopped spinach or kale. Continue cooking for another 2-3 minutes until the tomatoes become slightly tender and the greens wilt.

Crack and Whisk the Eggs:

Crack the eggs into a bowl and whisk them until the yolks and whites are well combined.

Pour the whisked eggs over the sautéed vegetables in the skillet.

Season gently:

Sprinkle a pinch of salt-free seasoning blend and freshly ground black pepper over the eggs. Be mindful of your sodium intake and adjust the seasoning accordingly.

Scramble:

Using a spatula, gently scramble and mix the eggs with the vegetables. Cook for about 2-3 minutes, or until the eggs are cooked to your desired level of doneness.

Serve:

Transfer the scramble to a plate. If desired, top with sliced avocado and fresh herbs like parsley or chives for extra flavor and nutrients.

Enjoy:

Sit down and savor your delicious low sodium breakfast.

Nutritional Benefits:

This low-sodium breakfast meal is rich in protein from the **eggs** and **vegetables,** and provides vitamins and minerals from the veggies. The **avocado** adds healthy fats and creaminess to the dish.

Add low-sodium seasonings or herbs to suit your taste.

Note:

If you want to reduce sodium even further, avoid using pre-made spice blends and sauces, as they often contain hidden sodium. Instead, opt for fresh herbs and homemade spice mixes.

6.3. Gluten-Free Banana Oat Pancakes for One

Description

This gluten-free pancake recipe is not only delicious but also offers dietary benefits. It's made with wholesome ingredients like oats and bananas, providing fiber and nutrients to start your day right.

Ingredients:

- 1/2 ripe banana
- 1/2 cup gluten-free rolled oats
- 1/4 cup unsweetened almond milk (or any milk of your choice)
- 1 large egg
- 1/2 teaspoon pure vanilla extract
- 1/2 teaspoon baking powder
- 1/4 teaspoon ground cinnamon
- Pinch of salt , (or salt free alternative)

- Cooking oil or cooking spray for the pan
- Fresh berries, sliced banana, or pure maple syrup for topping (optional)

Instructions:

Prepare the Batter:

In a blender or food processor, add the ripe banana, gluten-free rolled oats, almond milk, egg, vanilla extract, baking powder, ground cinnamon, and a pinch of salt (or an alternative).

Blend Until Smooth:

Blend the ingredients until you have a smooth pancake batter. This should take just a minute or two. Scrape down the sides of the blender as needed to ensure everything is well combined.

Preheat the Pan:

Heat a non-stick skillet or griddle over medium heat. Add a small amount of cooking oil or use cooking spray to prevent sticking.

Cook the Pancakes:

Pour 1/4 cup of the batter onto the heated skillet for each pancake. You can make one large pancake or a few smaller ones, depending on your preference.

Cook Until Bubbles Form:

Let the pancakes cook until bubbles form on the surface, and the edges start to look set, about 2-3 minutes.

Flip and Cook the Other Side:

Gently flip the pancakes and cook the other side for an additional 1-2 minutes, or until they are golden brown and cooked through.

Serve:

Transfer the pancakes to a plate. Top with fresh berries, sliced banana, or a drizzle of pure maple syrup if desired.

Enjoy:

These gluten-free banana oat pancakes are not only tasty but also packed with fiber from the oats and potassium from the bananas. They are a satisfying and nutritious way to start your day.

Nutritional Benefits

These gluten-free banana oat pancakes are packed with fiber from the **oats** and potassium from the **bananas**. They are a satisfying and nutritious way to start your day.

Note:

Ensure that the oats you use are labeled gluten-free if you have celiac disease or a severe gluten sensitivity to avoid cross-contamination.

Variations:

You can also add other mix-ins to the batter, such as chopped nuts, chocolate chips, or dried fruit, for added flavor and texture. Adjust the sweetness by using more or less banana or adding a sweetener of your choice to the batter if desired.

Appendix:

Conversion Charts and Kitchen Measurements

In the world of cooking, reasonably accurate measurements may be crucial for successful recipes. Whether converting units or needing to know how much of an ingredient to use, the following American based conversion charts and kitchen measurements guide will be a handy reference.

Volume Measurements:

1 teaspoon (tsp) = 5 milliliters (mL)

1 tablespoon (tbsp) = 20 milliliters (mL)

1 fluid ounce (fl oz) = 30 milliliters (mL)

1 cup (c) = 240 milliliters (mL)

1 pint (pt) = 480 milliliters (mL)

1 quart (qt) = 960 milliliters (mL)

1 gallon (gal) = 3.8 liters (L)

Weight Measurements:

1 ounce (oz) = 28 grams (g)

1 pound (lb) = 16 ounces (oz) = 453 grams (g)

1 kilogram (kg) = 1,000 grams (g) = 2.2 pounds (lb)

Dry Ingredients:

1 cup all-purpose flour = 120 grams

1 cup granulated sugar = 200 grams

1 cup brown sugar (packed) = 220 grams

1 cup powdered sugar = 120 grams

1 cup butter = 227 grams (2 sticks)

1 cup oats = 90 grams

Liquid Ingredients:

1 cup milk = 240 milliliters (mL)

1 cup water = 240 milliliters (mL)

1 cup vegetable oil = 240 milliliters (mL)

Temperature Conversions:

°F to °C: (°F - 32) × 5/9

°C to °F: (°C × 9/5) + 32

Oven Temperature:

275°F = 140°C (very low heat)

300°F = 150°C (low heat)

350°F = 180°C (moderate heat)

375°F = 190°C (moderate to high heat)

400°F = 200°C (high heat)

Common Kitchen Equivalents:

1 stick of butter = 1/2 cup = 8 tablespoons

1 lemon = approximately 2-3 tablespoons of juice

1 orange = approximately 1/2 cup of juice

1 medium onion = approximately 1 cup chopped

1 garlic clove = approximately 1/2 teaspoon minced

1 medium banana = approximately 1/2 cup mashed

These conversion charts and kitchen measurements are meant to assist you in your culinary endeavours, ensuring that your recipes turn out just the way you intend them to.

Printed in Dunstable, United Kingdom